VINCE STAPLES

The Complete Biography of a Hip-Hop Icon

Ashley D. Western

Table Of Contents

Introduction

Vincent Jamal Staples, born on July 2, 1993, is an American rapper and singer hailing from Long Beach, California. His journey to musical recognition began with his affiliation with the California-based alternative hip hop collective Odd Future, particularly with members Mike G and Earl Sweatshirt. Prior to gaining wider recognition, Staples signed with Talib Kweli's Blacksmith Records and collaborated with Mac Miller on the mixtape "Stolen Youth" (2013). Subsequently, he inked a deal with No I.D.'s ARTium Recordings, a Def Jam Recordings imprint, releasing his debut extended play, "Hell Can Wait" (2014), which marked his first entry onto the Billboard 200 chart.

Staples' ascent to prominence was propelled by his contributions to projects by fellow Odd Future members, such as Earl Sweatshirt's "Journey to the 5th Echelon" (2010) and "Doris" (2013). "Hell Can Wait" garnered critical acclaim, featuring standout singles like "Hands Up" and "Blue Suede." His debut album, "Summertime '06" (2015), continued the trend of positive reception and included the platinum-certified single "Norf Norf," solidifying his inclusion in the XXL 2015 Freshman Class. Subsequent albums, namely "Big Fish Theory" (2017), "FM!" (2019), his self-titled fourth studio album (2021), and "Ramona Park Broke My Heart" (2022), showcased Staples' evolving artistry, earning both critical acclaim and moderate commercial success. His musical style is often characterized as West Coast hip hop, featuring conscious themes, and experimenting with avant-garde, dance, and electronic influences.

Beyond his solo endeavors, Staples is a member of the California-based hip hop trio Cutthroat Boyz alongside Aston Matthews and Joey Fatts. In addition to his music career, he has ventured into acting, with notable roles in films like "Dope" and "White Men Can't Jump," as well as the television series "Abbott Elementary." As a voice actor, Staples lent his talents to the 2015 film "Mutafukaz" and animated series like "American Dad!" and "Lazor Wulf." In 2015, he expanded his professional portfolio by becoming a spokesperson and brand ambassador for Sprite.

Chapter 1: Early Life and Education

Birth and Childhood in Compton, California

Vince Staples, born Vincent Jamal Staples on July 2, 1993, began his life's journey in the iconic city of Compton, California. Compton, known for its rich cultural heritage and complex socio-economic landscape, served as the backdrop to Staples' formative years. Growing up in this environment exposed him to the realities of urban life, marked by both its vibrant energy and its challenges, particularly the high crime rates prevalent in the area.

Within the dynamic and often tumultuous setting of Compton, Vince Staples' childhood unfolded. His early experiences in the city would later shape his worldview and influence the narratives within his music. Compton's streets became the canvas on which Staples painted the vivid stories of resilience, struggle, and survival.

Family Background and Siblings

Vince Staples emerged as the youngest member in a family of five siblings, comprising two brothers and three sisters. The dynamics of a large family played a significant role in shaping Staples' character, providing him with a support system and a sense of shared experience. Raised in an environment marked by limited resources and economic challenges, Staples' family background contributed to the resilience that would become a hallmark of his persona.

The struggles and triumphs experienced within his family unit laid the groundwork for the thematic elements that would later emerge in his music. Staples' lyrics often draw from personal narratives, and his family background serves as a wellspring of inspiration for exploring themes of perseverance, familial bonds, and the pursuit of a better life.

Educational Journey: Optimal Christian Academy, High School Experiences

Vince Staples' educational odyssey commenced at Optimal Christian Academy, where he spent the crucial years from 4th to 8th grade. This period, marked by academic and personal growth, left an indelible imprint on the young Staples. Optimal Christian Academy not only provided an education but also fostered an environment that Staples often refers to as influential and positive.

However, high school brought a series of transitions for Vince Staples. His mother's decision to send him to Atlanta for six months to live with one of his sisters marked a pivotal change. This relocation presented Staples with an opportunity to experience a different cultural milieu and added layers to his understanding of the world.

Returning to Southern California, Staples navigated through various high schools, including Jordan High School in Long Beach, Mayfair High School in Lakewood, Opportunity High School for homeschooling, Esperanza High School in Anaheim, and Kennedy High School, among others. This diverse educational journey, characterized by constant change and adaptation, mirrors the broader narrative of Staples' life.

Staples has been forthright about his involvement with street gangs during his youth, acknowledging the challenges associated with this aspect of his life. Despite the hurdles, education remained a consistent thread. Staples became not only a storyteller through his music but also an advocate for steering youth away from the perils of the gang lifestyle.

In the realm of sports, Staples found solace and camaraderie. Participating in Snoop Dogg's Snoop Youth Football League (SYFL) provided him with a sense of community and shared purpose. The experience showcased the positive impact that influential figures like Snoop Dogg could have on the lives of young individuals.

Vince Staples' early life and educational journey laid the foundation for the artist he would become. Compton's challenges, coupled with the diverse educational experiences, contributed to shaping his unique perspective. These formative years sowed the seeds for the introspective, socially conscious artist who would later captivate audiences with his thought-provoking lyrics and authentic storytelling.

Chapter 2: Early Career (2009-2013)

Discovery by Dijon "LaVish" Samo and Chuck Wun

Vince Staples' entry into the music scene is a testament to the serendipitous nature of artistic discovery. It was in the hands of Dijon "LaVish" Samo and Chuck Wun that the budding talent of Vince Staples was unearthed. The journey began when LaVish took Staples on a trip to Los Angeles, where fate led him to cross paths with members of the influential Odd Future collective.

In the sprawling city of Los Angeles, Staples found himself in the company of notable figures within Odd Future, such as Syd tha Kyd, Mike G, and Earl Sweatshirt. Despite Staples not initially aspiring to become a rapper, his chance encounters during this trip set the stage for a significant shift in his trajectory. LaVish's role as a catalyst in introducing

Staples to the burgeoning world of Odd Future laid the groundwork for the artist's subsequent foray into the music industry.

Introduction to Odd Future Collective

Odd Future, short for Odd Future Wolf Gang Kill Them All, represented a collective of artists known for their avant-garde approach to hip hop. The group garnered attention for their unapologetic and unconventional style, and within this creative melting pot, Vince Staples found both collaborators and mentors. The association with Odd Future, and in particular, artists like Earl Sweatshirt, Mike G, and Syd tha Kyd, provided Staples with a platform to showcase his burgeoning talent.

Staples' involvement with Odd Future extended beyond chance encounters. He made guest appearances on several tracks, most notably featuring on "epaR" from Earl Sweatshirt's March 2010 mixtape, "Earl." The collaborative efforts on projects like "Journey to the 5th Echelon" (2010) and "Doris" (2013) further solidified his presence within the collective.

Collaboration with Mac Miller: Stolen Youth (2013)

The pivotal moment in Vince Staples' early career occurred when he crossed paths with another luminary in the hip hop scene, Mac Miller. Under the alias Larry Fisherman, Miller and Staples collaborated on a mixtape titled "Stolen Youth," released in June 2013. This collaborative effort showcased Staples' ability to seamlessly blend his lyrical prowess with Miller's distinctive production style.

"Stolen Youth" featured guest appearances from notable artists, including Miller himself, Ab-Soul, Schoolboy Q, Da$H, Hardo, and Staples' fellow Cutthroat Boyz member, Joey Fatts. The mixtape not only marked a significant milestone in Staples' discography but also served as a testament to his versatility as an artist.

The subsequent Space Migration Tour, where Staples joined Miller as a supporting act, provided a platform for his live performances and further solidified his presence in the hip hop circuit. The collaboration with Mac Miller not only expanded Staples' artistic horizons but also introduced him to a broader audience.

This chapter of Vince Staples' biography delves into the crucial years of 2009 to 2013, where chance encounters, collaborations, and introductions to influential collectives laid the groundwork for the artist's ascent. The Odd Future affiliation and the collaborative efforts with Mac Miller set the stage for Staples' emergence as a distinctive voice in the evolving landscape of hip hop.

Chapter 3: Rise to Prominence (2014-2015)

Signing with No I.D.'s ARTium Recordings

The turning point in Vince Staples' career came with a strategic move in 2014 when he signed with No I.D.'s ARTium Recordings, an imprint under the influential Def Jam Recordings. This alliance marked a significant step forward for Staples, aligning him with a label known for fostering groundbreaking talent in the hip hop industry.

No I.D., a seasoned producer and mentor, played a pivotal role in shaping Staples' artistic trajectory. The partnership not only provided him with a platform for creative expression but also set the stage for the release of his debut extended play (EP), "Hell Can Wait."

Debut EP: Hell Can Wait (2014)

"Hell Can Wait," released on October 7, 2014, marked Vince Staples' debut EP under the ARTium Recordings banner. The EP garnered critical acclaim, serving as an introduction to Staples' unique storytelling ability and unapologetic lyricism. Notable singles from the EP, including "Hands Up" and "Blue Suede," resonated with audiences and showcased Staples' capacity to address societal issues with a raw and poignant perspective.

The thematic depth of "Hell Can Wait" not only solidified Staples' reputation as a conscious rapper but also positioned him as an artist unafraid to confront challenging subject matter. The EP's success propelled Staples further into the spotlight, setting the stage for his subsequent projects.

Debut Album: Summertime '06 (2015)

The pinnacle of Vince Staples' early career came with the release of his debut studio album, "Summertime '06," on June 30, 2015. This ambitious double-disc album was a tour de force, exploring Staples' experiences and reflections on growing up in Long Beach, California.

"Summertime '06" received widespread acclaim for its authenticity, lyrical complexity, and the bold narrative it presented. Staples' storytelling prowess shone through in tracks like "Norf Norf," which achieved platinum certification and solidified his status as a potent force in West Coast hip hop. The album's success not only resonated with critics but also positioned Staples as a torchbearer for a new wave of conscious and introspective hip hop artists.

Inclusion in XXL 2015 Freshman Class

The year 2015 proved to be a defining period for Vince Staples as he earned a coveted spot in the XXL 2015 Freshman Class. This acknowledgment from one of the most respected publications in hip hop served as a testament to Staples' rapid ascent and undeniable impact on the genre.

The inclusion in the Freshman Class not only validated Staples' artistic merit but also positioned him among a select group of emerging artists destined for greatness. Alongside fellow up-and-coming rappers, Staples stood out as a distinctive voice, offering a refreshing blend of social commentary and artistic innovation.

This chapter encapsulates the crucial years of 2014 to 2015, where Staples, under the mentorship of No I.D., made strategic career moves that propelled him to new heights. The release of "Hell Can Wait" and the monumental success of "Summertime '06" firmly established Vince Staples as a force to be reckoned with in the ever-evolving landscape of hip hop.

Chapter 4: Artistic Evolution (2016-2017)

Prima Donna EP (2016)

The years 2016 and 2017 marked a transformative phase in Vince Staples' career, characterized by an unparalleled artistic evolution. At the forefront of this evolution was the release of the EP "Prima Donna" on August 25, 2016. This seven-track project showcased Staples' willingness to push the boundaries of conventional hip hop, exploring new sonic landscapes and thematic depth.

"Prima Donna" was more than just a musical endeavor; it was an audiovisual experience accompanied by a thought-provoking short film. Staples, in collaboration with acclaimed director Nabil Elderkin, created a visual narrative that complemented the EP's sonic experimentation. This interdisciplinary approach underscored Staples' commitment to elevating his craft beyond the confines of traditional music releases.

Big Fish Theory (2017)

The apex of Vince Staples' artistic evolution during this period came with the release of his sophomore studio album, "Big Fish Theory," on June 23, 2017. This album defied genre norms, seamlessly blending hip hop with avant-garde, electronic, and dance influences. Staples, in collaboration with leading producers like SOPHIE and Flume, crafted a sonic tapestry that challenged preconceived notions of what West Coast hip hop could sound like.

"Big Fish Theory" wasn't just an album; it was a sonic manifesto. Staples delved into themes of fame, self-discovery, and the tumultuous nature of the music industry. Tracks like "BagBak" and "Big Fish" became anthems that resonated not only with hip hop enthusiasts but also with a broader audience appreciative of innovative and boundary-pushing music.

This project showcased Staples' commitment to staying ahead of the curve, refusing to be confined by the expectations set by his earlier successes. "Big Fish Theory" was a critical triumph, earning widespread acclaim for its bold experimentation and cementing Staples' reputation as a maverick in the hip hop landscape.

Collaborations and Features

In addition to his solo endeavors, Vince Staples continued to make waves through collaborations and features. Notably, he lent his distinctive voice to the Gorillaz track "Ascension," featured on their 2017 album "Humanz." This collaboration underscored Staples' versatility as an artist capable of seamlessly integrating into diverse musical landscapes.

Staples' collaborative spirit extended beyond the realm of music, as he joined forces with acclaimed film composer Hans Zimmer. Their remix of the UEFA Champions League Anthem for the FIFA 19 reveal trailer demonstrated Staples' ability to transcend traditional musical boundaries and venture into uncharted territories.

This part encapsulates a crucial period of artistic growth for Vince Staples. The "Prima Donna" EP and "Big Fish Theory" not only solidified his position as an innovator but also showcased his commitment to pushing the envelope of what hip hop could achieve. Collaborations with iconic figures like Gorillaz and Hans Zimmer affirmed Staples' place as a multifaceted artist unafraid to explore new frontiers in both music and beyond.

Chapter 5: Continued Success (2018-Present)

FM! (2018)

The years following the groundbreaking "Big Fish Theory" saw Vince Staples navigate the ever-changing landscape of the music industry with finesse and innovation. In 2018, he unveiled his third studio album, "FM!" on November 2. Departing from the expansive experimentation of its predecessor, "FM!" paid homage to the raw and unapologetic essence of West Coast hip hop.

The album, presented in the format of a radio show, seamlessly blended tracks with witty interludes, creating a cohesive listening experience. Staples, always the storyteller, used this format to paint a vivid picture of Long Beach, California, and share his unique perspective on the cultural and social dynamics of the region.

The Vince Staples Show

Parallel to his musical endeavors, Vince Staples ventured into the realm of digital content with "The Vince Staples Show." Launched in 2019, this web series provided fans with a window into Staples' irreverent sense of humor and sharp social commentary. The show, consisting of short episodes, featured skits, interviews, and, at times, unexpected celebrity cameos. "The Vince Staples Show" became a platform for Staples to express himself beyond the confines of his music, showcasing his versatility as an entertainer.

Self-Titled Album (2021)

Staples continued his trajectory of artistic evolution with the release of his self-titled album on July 9, 2021. The album served as a testament to his ability to navigate various sonic landscapes while staying true to his Long Beach roots. Tracks like "Law of Averages" and "Are You With That?" demonstrated a nuanced blend of introspective lyricism and infectious beats, reaffirming Staples' status as a lyrical force in contemporary hip hop.

Ramona Park Broke My Heart (2022)

In 2022, Vince Staples unveiled "Ramona Park Broke My Heart," an EP that further underscored his commitment to pushing creative boundaries. The EP, released on February 18, featured collaborations with artists like Lil Jon and Pharell Williams, showcasing a fusion of Staples' distinctive style with diverse musical influences.

This chapter illuminates Vince Staples' journey through the latter part of the 2010s and into the 2020s. "FM!" and the self-titled album demonstrated his ability to adapt and innovate within the hip hop landscape. Meanwhile, "The Vince Staples Show" provided fans with an intimate glimpse into his personality, expanding his presence beyond the music scene. The self-titled album and "Ramona Park Broke My Heart" further solidified Vince

Staples' position as a dynamic and influential figure in contemporary hip hop.

Chapter 6: Other Ventures

Cutthroat Boyz

As Vince Staples continued to ascend the ranks in the hip hop realm, he found himself involved in various collaborative projects. One notable venture was the formation of the hip hop trio Cutthroat Boyz, consisting of Staples, Joey Fatts, and Aston Matthews. The group, emerging from the vibrant Los Angeles rap scene, brought a distinct energy and gritty authenticity to their music. Their collaborative efforts, including mixtapes like "Cutthroat Boyz" and "CUTTHROAT RADIO," showcased a camaraderie that extended beyond individual artistry.

Acting Career

Beyond the mic, Vince Staples ventured into the realm of acting, proving his versatility as a multi-faceted artist. His foray into acting began with a memorable role in the 2015 film "Dope," directed by Rick Famuyiwa. In the film, Staples played the character Dom, a charismatic and street-savvy individual who added depth to the narrative.

Staples continued to make waves in the film industry with his involvement in the 2017 sports comedy "White Men Can't Jump," a remake of the classic 1992 film. This marked a significant step in his acting career, showcasing his ability to transition seamlessly between the worlds of music and film.

One of his notable recent ventures in the acting realm was his involvement in the TV series "Abbott Elementary." The comedy series, set in a Philadelphia public school, featured Staples in a recurring role, adding a dose of his unique charisma to the small screen.

Voice Acting

Expanding his creative horizons, Vince Staples delved into the realm of voice acting, leaving an indelible mark in animated projects. In the animated film "Mutafukaz" (2017), Staples lent his voice to the character of Vinz, contributing to the film's urban and edgy aesthetic.

Staples also made appearances in popular animated TV series, such as "American Dad!" and "Lazor Wulf." His voice acting roles showcased a different facet of his artistic expression, allowing fans to appreciate his distinctive voice and storytelling abilities in a new context.

This chapter illuminates Vince Staples' ventures beyond the music studio, showcasing his collaborative spirit in Cutthroat Boyz, his evolving acting career, and his exploration of voice acting. Staples' ability to seamlessly transition between music and various forms of entertainment underscores his status as a multifaceted artist, continually expanding his impact on popular culture.

Chapter 7: Philanthropy and Personal Life

Involvement in Street Gangs and Outreach to Youth

Vince Staples, hailing from the streets of Compton, California, carries a narrative deeply intertwined with the realities of inner-city life. Raised in an environment where street gangs exerted a profound influence, Staples was not immune to the challenges presented by his surroundings. His early exposure to gang culture served as a backdrop to his music, infusing it with raw authenticity and a keen awareness of societal issues.

As his career soared, Staples remained connected to his roots, using his platform to address the struggles faced by many in similar circumstances. His outreach to the youth, particularly those entangled in the complex web of street life, became a focal point of his philanthropic efforts. By sharing his own experiences, he aimed to provide guidance and inspiration, encouraging young individuals to navigate away from the pitfalls of gang life and pursue positive avenues for personal growth.

Philanthropic Activities: YMCA Program

Vince Staples' commitment to making a positive impact on his community is exemplified through his involvement in philanthropic activities. One notable initiative is his support for YMCA programs, which focus on providing opportunities and resources for young people. Staples understands the transformative power of mentorship and structured programs, recognizing them as essential tools in steering youth away from negative influences.

His contributions to the YMCA program underscore his dedication to creating tangible change and fostering an environment where young individuals can thrive. By investing in such initiatives, Staples actively participates in building a foundation for a brighter future for the next generation.

Personal Lifestyle Choices: Straight Edge, Sports, Fandoms

Beyond the spotlight, Vince Staples maintains a distinct personal lifestyle that reflects his values and preferences. One notable aspect is his adherence to the Straight Edge philosophy. This lifestyle choice involves abstaining from alcohol, recreational drugs, and other vices commonly associated with the music industry. Staples' commitment to the Straight Edge lifestyle is a testament to his focus on maintaining a clear and sober mindset, ensuring his artistic vision remains uncompromised.

Sports also play a significant role in Staples' personal life. Whether expressing his passion for basketball or engaging with other athletic pursuits, he finds a source of inspiration and recreation in the world of sports. This facet of his life not only adds depth to his persona but also provides a balance to the intensity of his creative endeavors.

Moreover, Staples is known for his engagement with various fandoms, showcasing a more playful and relatable side. Whether expressing his love for particular movies, TV shows, or other forms of entertainment, his interactions with fandoms demonstrate the diverse facets of his personality beyond the music scene.

This chapter delves into Vince Staples' commitment to making a positive impact on his community, addressing the challenges associated with street life, and his multifaceted personal lifestyle choices. Staples emerges not only as a talented artist but also as a conscientious individual actively contributing to the betterment of society and embodying a well-rounded and principled approach to life.

Chapter 8: Corporate Sponsorship and Endorsements

Partnership with Sprite

Vince Staples, a prominent figure in the hip-hop landscape, transcends the boundaries of music, extending his influence into the realm of corporate partnerships and endorsements. One notable collaboration that stands out in this chapter of his career is his partnership with Sprite. This strategic alliance goes beyond the conventional realms of celebrity endorsements, reflecting Staples' unique appeal and the alignment of his brand with Sprite's image.

The partnership with Sprite not only underscores Staples' marketability but also speaks to the cultural significance of his persona. As a refreshingly authentic artist, Staples resonates with Sprite's commitment to individuality and self-expression. The collaboration extends beyond mere promotional efforts; it intertwines the essence of Staples' artistry with the brand's identity, creating a synergy that goes beyond the surface level of typical celebrity endorsements.

Staples' involvement with Sprite is not confined to conventional advertising. The collaboration extends into the creative sphere, where Staples, known for his innovative approach to music videos and visual storytelling, brings a fresh perspective to Sprite's marketing campaigns. The result is a fusion of artistic expression and commercial appeal, a testament to Staples' ability to seamlessly integrate his creative vision into corporate collaborations.

Collaboration with Acura on Next-Gen Integra Campaign

In the ever-evolving landscape of hip-hop, artists are increasingly becoming influential figures not only in music but also in shaping broader cultural trends. Vince Staples, recognizing the intersection of music and lifestyle, ventured into collaborations with renowned brands, including his partnership with Acura on the Next-Gen Integra campaign.

The collaboration with Acura represents Staples' foray into the automotive industry, a move that aligns with the expanding role of musicians as cultural tastemakers. The Next-Gen Integra campaign, featuring Staples, not only highlights the sleek design and performance of the vehicle but also reflects a mutual understanding between the artist and the brand. Staples' distinct style and forward-thinking approach resonate with Acura's commitment to innovation and sophistication.

Beyond the traditional realms of endorsement, Staples actively engages with the creative process of the campaign, contributing his artistic vision to the representation of the Next-Gen Integra. This collaborative effort goes beyond a transactional celebrity endorsement, establishing a meaningful partnership where the artist's influence permeates the brand's narrative.

This part delves into Vince Staples' ventures into corporate sponsorship and endorsements, exploring the intricacies of his collaborations with Sprite and Acura. Beyond the commercial aspect, these partnerships reveal a nuanced understanding of the intersection between artistic expression, individuality, and corporate identity. Staples, as an artist, not only endorses products but also contributes his creativity to these collaborations, leaving an indelible mark on the evolving landscape of celebrity endorsements in the contemporary music industry.

Chapter 9: Discography

Overview of Studio Albums, EPs, and Mixtapes

Vince Staples' discography stands as a testament to his evolution as an artist, showcasing a dynamic range that transcends the boundaries of traditional hip-hop. This chapter delves into the comprehensive overview of Staples' studio albums, EPs, and mixtapes, providing insights into the artistic progression that defines his musical journey.

Studio Albums

- **Summertime '06 (2015):** Staples' debut studio album, "Summertime '06," emerges as a raw and introspective exploration of his experiences growing up in Long Beach, California. The double-disc album garnered critical acclaim for its unfiltered lyricism and production.

- **Big Fish Theory (2017):** A departure from conventional hip-hop norms, "Big Fish Theory" solidifies Staples' reputation as an avant-garde artist. The album incorporates electronic and experimental elements, showcasing his willingness to push the boundaries of the genre.

- **FM! (2018):** "FM!" takes a different approach, presenting itself as a radio show with succinct tracks. Staples combines sharp social commentary with infectious beats, creating a project that resonates with both casual listeners and dedicated fans.

- **Vince Staples (2021): The self-titled album** marks a return to Staples' roots, featuring a more stripped-down and personal exploration of his life and perspective. It serves as a reflection on his journey in the music industry and the challenges he has faced.

- **Ramona Park Broke My Heart (2022):** This EP further enriches Staples' discography, offering a compact yet potent collection of tracks. It serves as a bridge between his previous works and the anticipation of what the future holds for the artist.

EPs

- **Hell Can Wait (2014):** Staples' debut EP, "Hell Can Wait," precedes his first studio album and provides a glimpse into the thematic elements that would later define his discography.

- **Prima Donna (2016):** This EP serves as a conceptual piece, delving into the psychological aspects of fame and its impact on an artist's mental state.

Mixtapes:

- **Shyne Coldchain Vol. 1 (2011):** A precursor to his major-label success, this mixtape showcases Staples' early lyrical prowess and sets the stage for his future endeavors.

- **Stolen Youth (2013):** The collaborative mixtape with Mac Miller, "Stolen Youth," marks a significant moment in Staples' career, highlighting his ability to work seamlessly with other artists.

Notable Singles and Collaborations

In addition to his studio albums and mixtapes, Vince Staples has left an indelible mark on the hip-hop landscape through notable singles and collaborations. This section explores key tracks that have contributed to his prominence in the music industry, showcasing his versatility and ability to collaborate across genres.

- **"Norf Norf" (2015):** A standout single from "Summertime '06," "Norf Norf" gained attention for its unapologetic depiction of Staples' upbringing in North Long Beach.

- **"Big Fish" (2017):** The lead single from "Big Fish Theory," this track fuses electronic and hip-hop elements, becoming a symbol of Staples' innovative approach to music.

- **"FUN!" (2018):** A single from the "FM!" album, "FUN!" encapsulates Staples' ability to infuse social commentary into infectious beats, making a statement on the state of society.

- **"LAW OF AVERAGES" (2021):** Released as part of the self-titled album, this single reflects Staples' matured perspective and continued exploration of personal and societal themes.

- **"MAGIC" (2022):** A lead single from the "Ramona Park Broke My Heart" EP, "MAGIC" exemplifies Staples' lyrical dexterity and his capacity to deliver impactful narratives in concise formats.

This chapter gives a comprehensive overview to Vince Staples' discography, encapsulating the essence of each album, EP, and mixtape, along with highlighting the impact of his notable singles and collaborations. From his early days with "Shyne Coldchain Vol. 1" to the more recent self-titled album, Staples' musical journey unfolds as a rich tapestry of artistic exploration and innovation within the hip-hop genre.

Chapter 10: Concert Tours

Headlining Tours

Vince Staples' impact on the music industry extends beyond the studio, as evidenced by his electrifying performances on various concert tours. This chapter navigates through the headlining tours where Staples took center stage, captivating audiences with his commanding stage presence and delivering performances that transcended mere musical experiences.

- **Circa '06 Tour (2015):** In support of his debut album "Summertime '06," Staples embarked on the Circa '06 Tour, providing fans with an immersive live rendition of the raw and unapologetic tracks that defined the album. The tour showcased Staples' ability to bring the intensity of his studio recordings to the stage.

- **The Life Aquatic Tour (2017):** Following the release of "Big Fish Theory," Staples launched The Life Aquatic Tour, named after the Wes Anderson film. This tour not only highlighted tracks from the new album but also demonstrated Staples' evolving stage production, incorporating visual elements that complemented the experimental nature of the music.

- **Smile, You're on Camera Tour (2019):** With the release of "FM!," Staples embarked on the Smile, You're on Camera Tour. This tour embraced the radio show concept of the album, creating a dynamic live experience that mirrored the diversity of the project. Staples engaged audiences with his charismatic performance style, making each show a memorable event.

- **The Vince Staples Show Tour (2021):** To promote his self-titled album, Staples launched The Vince Staples Show Tour. This tour not only featured tracks from the latest album but also incorporated elements from his broader discography. Staples' ability to curate a setlist that resonated with both longtime fans and new listeners was evident throughout the tour.

Supporting Acts for Other Artists

In addition to headlining his own tours, Vince Staples has also lent his talents as a supporting act for other prominent artists. This section explores key instances where Staples took the stage in a supporting role, contributing to the overall energy of diverse concert line-ups.

- **Yeezus Tour with Kanye West (2013-2014):** Early in his career, Staples joined Kanye West as a supporting act on the Yeezus Tour. This experience exposed him to larger audiences and established him as an artist capable of holding his own on major stages.

- **The Life of Pablo Tour with Kanye West (2016):** Building on the success of the Yeezus Tour, Staples once again joined Kanye West, this time for The Life of Pablo Tour. The exposure gained from these tours with a hip-hop icon like Kanye West undoubtedly played a role in elevating Staples' profile within the industry.

- **Endless Summer Tour with G-Eazy and Logic (2016):** Collaborating with fellow artists G-Eazy and Logic, Staples brought his unique style to the Endless Summer Tour. The tour showcased the versatility of Staples as he seamlessly integrated into a lineup that spanned different sub-genres of hip-hop.

Vince Staples' live performances have become synonymous with energy, authenticity, and a commitment to delivering an unforgettable experience for his audience. Whether headlining his own tours or supporting other iconic artists, Staples' contributions to the live music scene have solidified his status as a captivating performer with a dynamic stage presence.

Chapter 11: Filmography

Vince Staples' artistic talents extend beyond the realm of music, with notable contributions to the world of film and television. This chapter delves into Staples' ventures in the entertainment industry, exploring his roles in films and television, as well as his accomplishments in the realm of voice acting.

Roles in Films and Television

- **Dope (2015):** Staples made his acting debut in the critically acclaimed film "Dope," directed by Rick Famuyiwa. The coming-of-age comedy-drama allowed Staples to showcase his versatility by taking on the role of Dom, a character whose complexities added depth to the narrative.

- **White Men Can't Jump (TBA):** Staples' involvement in the upcoming film "White Men Can't Jump" marks a significant step in his acting career. The film, a remake of the

1992 classic, positions Staples alongside other accomplished actors, signaling his continued growth in the world of cinema.

- **Abbott Elementary (2021–Present):** Staples ventured into television with a recurring role in the comedy series "Abbott Elementary." His portrayal of himself in the show, which revolves around the lives of teachers in a struggling Philadelphia school, adds a touch of authenticity to the comedic storyline.

Voice Acting Credits

- **Mutafukaz (2017):** Staples lent his voice to the English-language version of the animated film "Mutafukaz." His voice acting skills brought life to the character of Vinz, contributing to the film's unique blend of animation and urban storytelling.

- **American Dad! (2019–Present):** Staples extended his voice acting repertoire with a recurring role in the animated television series "American Dad!" His contributions to the show further showcase his ability to diversify his artistic expressions beyond traditional mediums.

- **Lazor Wulf (2019–Present):** Staples continued to make waves in the world of animation as he took on a voice acting role in the animated series "Lazor Wulf." His involvement in the show aligns with the industry's recognition of his distinctive voice and ability to infuse characters with personality.

Vince Staples' foray into film and television underscores his multidimensional artistic prowess. From bringing authenticity to on-screen characters to infusing life into animated roles, Staples' contributions to the visual storytelling landscape further solidify his status as a creative force to be reckoned with in the entertainment industry.

Chapter 12: Awards and Nominations

Vince Staples' journey in the music industry has been marked by critical acclaim and recognition, as evidenced by his presence in various award shows and the accumulation of notable achievements. This chapter explores Staples' impact on the awards circuit, shedding light on the accolades he has received and the milestones that have contributed to his standing as a respected artist.

Recognition in Award Shows

Grammy Awards:

- **Best Rap Album (2016):** Staples garnered his first Grammy nomination for his debut double-disc album, "Summertime '06." The nomination solidified his position as a noteworthy figure in the rap scene, earning recognition from one of the most prestigious award ceremonies in the music industry.

BET Hip Hop Awards:

- **Best Mixtape (2015):** Staples' mixtape, "Shyne Coldchain Vol. 2," received acclaim in the form of a BET Hip Hop Award nomination. The acknowledgment highlighted his prowess not only in studio albums but also in the mixtape format, showcasing his versatility as an artist.

MTV Europe Music Awards:

- **Best Video (2015):** The MTV EMA nomination for "Norf Norf," a single from the debut album "Summertime '06," emphasized Staples' impact beyond the borders of the United States. The international recognition underscored the global appeal of his music.

Notable Achievements

- **XXL Freshman Class (2015):** Staples' inclusion in the XXL Freshman Class of 2015 served as a pivotal moment in his career. This acknowledgment by the influential hip-hop publication marked him as one of the promising talents to watch, solidifying his presence in the ever-evolving landscape of hip-hop.

- **Critical Acclaim for "Summertime '06" (2015):** Staples' debut studio album, "Summertime '06," received widespread critical acclaim for its storytelling, production, and overall artistic vision. The album's positive reviews contributed to Staples' reputation as a lyrically skilled and innovative artist.

- **Vince Staples Day (2019):** The city of Long Beach honored Staples by declaring July 7, 2019, as Vince Staples Day. This recognition not only celebrated his contributions to music but also acknowledged his impact on the local community, solidifying his status as a hometown hero.

Vince Staples' journey in the music industry has been punctuated by nominations from prestigious award shows and notable achievements that speak to his influence and innovation. As he continues to push artistic boundaries, his presence on the awards stage remains a testament to his enduring impact on the world of music.

Conclusion

Vince Staples, a luminary in the realm of hip-hop, has left an indelible mark on the music and entertainment industry. From his humble beginnings in Compton, California, to becoming a Grammy-nominated artist and a cultural force, Staples' journey reflects not only personal growth but also a commitment to authenticity and artistic evolution.

Staples' early life and education set the stage for a narrative steeped in resilience and determination. Growing up in Compton, he navigated the challenges of his environment while forging a path through education. The chapters on his early career, rise to prominence, and artistic evolution illuminate the trajectory of an artist unafraid to explore diverse musical landscapes, collaborating with industry heavyweights and delivering projects that defy genre boundaries.

His continued success, marked by albums like "FM!" and "Vince Staples," as well as ventures like "The Vince Staples Show," showcases an artist with a keen sense of innovation and a willingness to push creative boundaries. Staples' ability to connect with audiences through his music and storytelling is a testament to his unique voice in an industry constantly in flux.

Beyond the mic, Staples' foray into acting, voice acting, and philanthropy further underscores his multifaceted talent and commitment to making a positive impact. His involvement in outreach programs and dedication to a straight-edge lifestyle demonstrate a desire to uplift his community and inspire the next generation.

In the corporate realm, Staples' partnerships with brands like Sprite and collaborations on campaigns, such as the Next-Gen Integra with Acura, highlight his influence not only in music but also in the world of endorsements and sponsorships.

As we delve into Vince Staples' discography, concert tours, filmography, and the recognition he has received through awards and nominations, it becomes evident that his journey is a tapestry woven with diverse threads of talent, resilience, and a genuine connection with his audience.

In conclusion, Vince Staples stands not just as a rapper but as a cultural icon who has redefined the possibilities within the hip-hop genre. His impact extends far beyond the stage, reflecting a commitment to authenticity, innovation, and community upliftment. As the chapters of his career continue to unfold, Vince Staples remains a beacon of inspiration for aspiring artists and a testament to the transformative power of music.

Made in the USA
Las Vegas, NV
20 May 2024

90142891R00036